TICKLE YOUR BRAIN

Mummy Mania!

First published in the UK in 2011 by The Salariya Book Company Ltd
This edition published in the UK in 2024 by Hatch Press,
an imprint of Bonnier Books UK
4th Floor, Victoria House
Bloomsbury Square, London WC1B 4DA
Owned by Bonnier Books
Sveavägen 56, Stockholm, Sweden
www.bonnierbooks.co.uk

1 3 5 7 9 10 8 6 4 2

ISBN 978-1-80078-850-3

Printed in the United Kingdom

MIX
Paper | Supporting
responsible forestry
FSC
www.fsc.org
FSC® C018072

TICKLE YOUR BRAIN
FACTS AND JOKES

Mummy Mania!

Hatch

INTRODUCTION

This gory history book is all about real mummies in real museums across the globe. Yes, it covers the weird, wacky, yucky world of mummification. The hundreds of places that store or display mummies can reveal fascinating, strange and disgusting secrets about human life and death!

There are spooky stories to tell, curses to be unwrapped, and suprising scientific techniques to be revealed. This book is a little bit like a mummy's coffin itself — stuffed with all the revolting bits, ready for you to unravel! Be prepared to be unprepared...

In Egypt, where history's deep,
A rat found old scrolls in a heap.
He read ancient tales,
Of boats and of sails,
And thought,
"I'll write a book that's unique!"

WHAT IS A MUMMY?

Any dead body, human or animal, that hasn't rotted is a mummy. To be mummified, a body is simply preserved, either intentionally or by accident. Artificial mummies are usually created to honour the dead, but natural mummies can occur spontaneously through unusual conditions. In both cases, the dead body does not decay and become a skeleton, as the skin (or fur) and flesh are preserved.

You name it, we'll mummify it.

Artificial mummies were made deliberately by people in different civilisations. They used various processes, such as drying the body out with natron and emptying their organs into special jars.

Natural mummies are created accidentally by nature – through drying, freezing, or other natural processes. Some accidental mummies can be very old.

What do you call an artificial mummy?
A phony pharaoh!

Why was an ancient mummy found at the bottom of a well?
It was an accident waiting to happen.

Which Egyptian Pharaoh was the most judgemental?
King Tut Tut!

WHERE DOES THE WORD 'MUMMY' COME FROM?

'Mummy' comes from the Arabic word *mummiya* which means pitch or wax (bitumen). Originally, people believed pitch or wax was the stuff responsible for the lasting mummification effects, based on the blackened state of the mummies' bodies. In actuality, most ancient Egyptians covered their dead in layers of dark resins, giving their skin a dark colour.

DID YOU KNOW?

All kinds of animals can become mummies. At the Smithsonian Museum in Washington, you can find mummies of bulls, cats, ibises (sacred Egyptian wading birds), hawks, crocodiles, dogs, and even baboons.

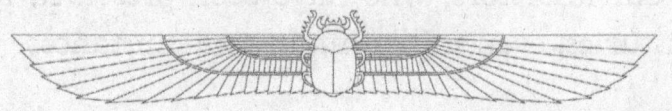

Other animals have been mummified naturally in bogs, pits or frozen soil. In August 2010, a mummified woolly mammoth nearly 40,000 years old was found in the Russian ice. Even its brain and blood vessels were perfectly mummified, allowing scientists to discover rare information from the past.

MUMMIES ON THE MOVE

For over 200 years people have flocked to see mummies in museums. Such eerie remains weren't just seen as spooky, but also fascinating and mysteriously exotic. The mummies in museums allow humans to catch a rare glimpse of our ancestors, who have been preserved for centuries, even millennia in some instances.

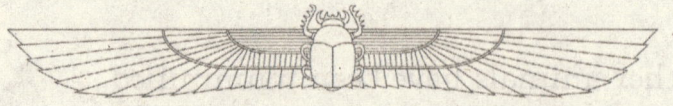

Q: How did the Pharaoh get to school?
A: In Aubis!

Knock, knock.
    Who's there?
Hieroglyph.
    Hieroglyph who?
You need to speak ancient Egyptian to get this joke!

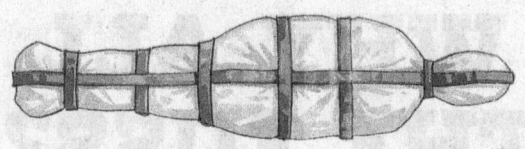

It has only been in more recent years that we have begun asking ethical questions about the plundering of ancient tombs and displaying the long dead. Is it right to place 'gruesome relics' in museums for the public to gawp at? Today, some mummies have been hidden away and are now kept out of sight as a sign of respect. What do you think about that?

Patient: Doctor, Doctor, I think I'm turning into a mummy!

Doctor: Don't worry, you're just a little bit wrapped up in yourself!

Patient: Doctor, Doctor, I've been feeling really stiff and old!

Doctor: Maybe you need to see a Cairo-practor!

WHY ALL THE FUSS?

When archaeologists first began finding ancient human mummies, there was great excitement. Mummies were often buried with treasures from the past, such as anicent amulets, jewels, masks and coins.

I'm not too sure about my birthday present, dear...

There were many mysteries to solve, but also money to be made. Rich people wanted to own not only the treasures, but also the mummies themselves. One hundred and fifty years ago, you could make a fortune by digging up mummies and selling them all around the world. Mummies became big business.

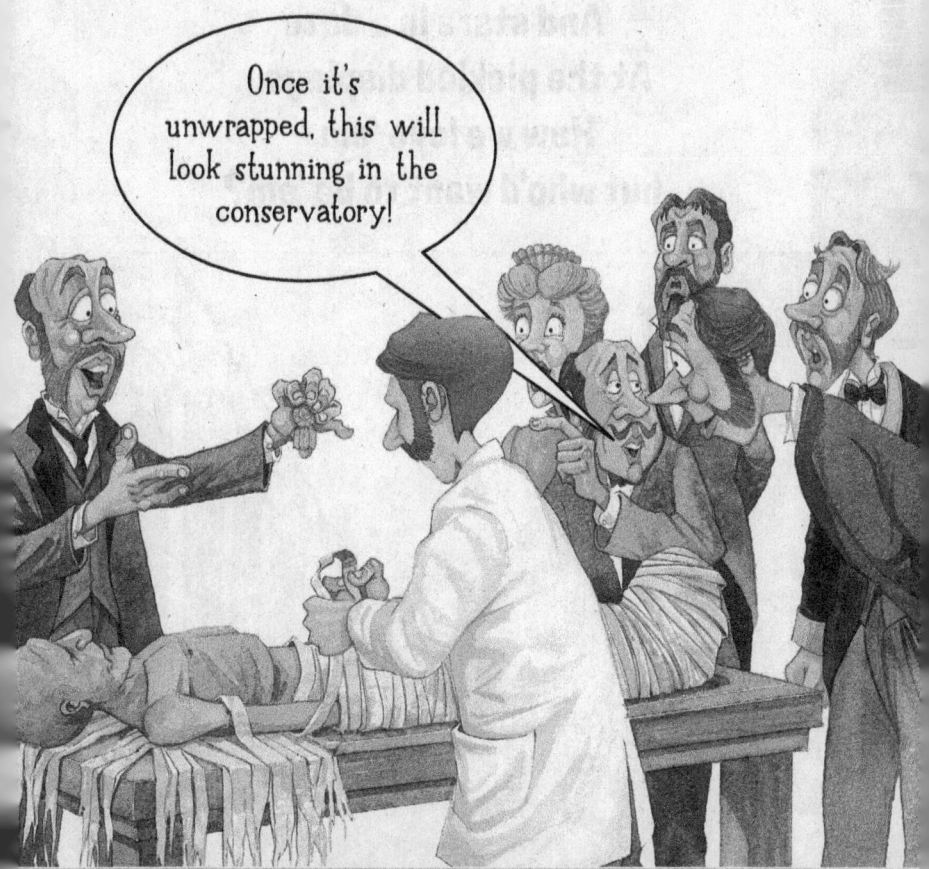

MUMMY LIMERICK

When mummies lie in a museum,
Huge crowds will queue up
just to see 'em
And stare in a daze
At the pickled displays...
How we love 'em –
but who'd want to be 'em?

SIX MUMMY RIDDLES

Q: During which age did the mummies first live?
A: The band-age

Q: What is a mummy's favourite kind of coffee?
A: De-coffin-ated

Q: What did the sign in the Egyptian museum
say?
A: 'Satisfaction guaranteed or your mummy back.'

Q: What's a mummy's favourite type of music?
A: Wrap music!

Q: Why don't mummies go on holiday?
A: They're afraid they'll relax and unwind!

Q: How do mummies send letters?
A: Through the ghost office

In a dark museum cellar
Lurks an ancient
cobweb dweller,
Tucked up in its tomb,
But now in the gloom...
It stirs... Eeek!
...oh, it's just the cleaner, Stella!

Opened in 1753, the British Museum in London was one of the first museums to display Ancient Egyptian treasures. It has one of the largest and most comprehensive collections of Egyptian artifacts in the world.

The Rosetta Stone, which was key to deciphering Egyptian hieroglyphs, has been in the British Museum since 1802. It was found during a dig in 1799, during Napoleon's campaign in Egypt.

THE MUSEUM...

The British Museum even has a cat mummy! Ancient Egyptians loved cats so much that they mummified them to keep as pets in the afterlife.

The Mummy Museum in Guanajuato, Mexico, has naturally mummified bodies. The dry climate of the area preserved these bodies almost by accident, and now they're on display.

The Louvre Museum in Paris has a mummy that is over 4,000 years old!

**Beware of museums
where mummies are kept.
No one who stayed overnight ever slept
Where bodies reside,
lit by moonlight...
Waiting to stir
in the cold DEAD of night.**

ONE DAY IN THE MUMMY MUSEUM...

'And this mummy over here,' croaked the 90-year-old museum guide, 'is five thousand, sixty-nine and a half years old. On its left, you can see another mummy which is four thousand and sixty-nine years and six months old.'

'Wow! That's amazing,' said a little lad in the audience, 'how can you age it so accurately to the exact month?'

'Well that's simple,' answered the old fellow, 'One was five thousand years old and the other was four thousand years old when I started working here 69½ years ago.'

ROTTEN FACTS

Turn the page now if you don't like smelly science! It's all about life, death and rotters. Yes, dead bodies rot because of all the micro-organisms (like bacteria) that chomp away on skin and flesh, or nibble away from the inside on all those gooey organs. Under 'normal' conditions, a dead body will start to decompose in just a few days and after only months, little more than bones remain. But sometimes a dead body won't decay at all. If no air, moisture and micro-organisms can get to work on a corpse, it can last indefinitely.

Help – I'm being pickled!

TWO ARCHAEOLOGISTS ARE EXCAVATING A TOMB IN EGYPT...

Arch I: I just found another tomb of a mummified pharaoh.

Arch 2:   Are you serious?

Arch I: No bones about it!

Arch 2:   It looks like the mummy is covered in chocolate and nuts.

Arch I: In that case, it must be Pharaoh Rocher.

Arch 2:	Do you like working with mummies?
Arch I:	Of corpse.
Arch 2:	So why are you crying as you sift through the rubble of this pyramid?
Arch I:	Because my work is in ruins. It's a dead-end job.

I've just dug up a tomb with its own toilet.

It must be a pee-ramid!

DON'T LOSE YOUR MUMMY

Shock horror – many mummies are vanishing! Some mummies are disappearing because they have not been preserved well over the years, compromising their integrity. Bright lights, damp, temperature fluctuations, and even insect damage can cause these ancient wonders to crumble into dust.

At least this stops me from getting sunburn!

Other mummies are disappearing from public view due to complaints that they're either too gross, or that the practice of displaying dead bodies is objectifying. Even ancient mummies are being removed from some museums, especially in the United States and across Europe. Yet many archaeologists still believe mummies have a place in museums. They argue that mummies can provide important insights into lost civilisations – as well as teaching about death itself.

Q: What did the Pharaoh say when he walked into the toilet?
A: Ugh, what SPHINX in here?!

Q: Why did the mummy become a detective?
A: Because it was an expert at unravelling things!

ANCIENT EGYPTIANS

The most famous mummies we know about today are undoubtedly the pharaohs of ancient Egypt, who lived aorund 3000 to 5000 years ago. Egyptians believed that the pharaoh was a living god who needed to be kept happy in life and remembered long after death. The Egyptians believed in an afterlife, so it was important to preserve each pharaoh in the best condition possible, ready for the next life. This was done by drying out the body and wrapping it tightly in linen bandages, to stop the rot setting in.

HOW TO BECOME A MUMMY

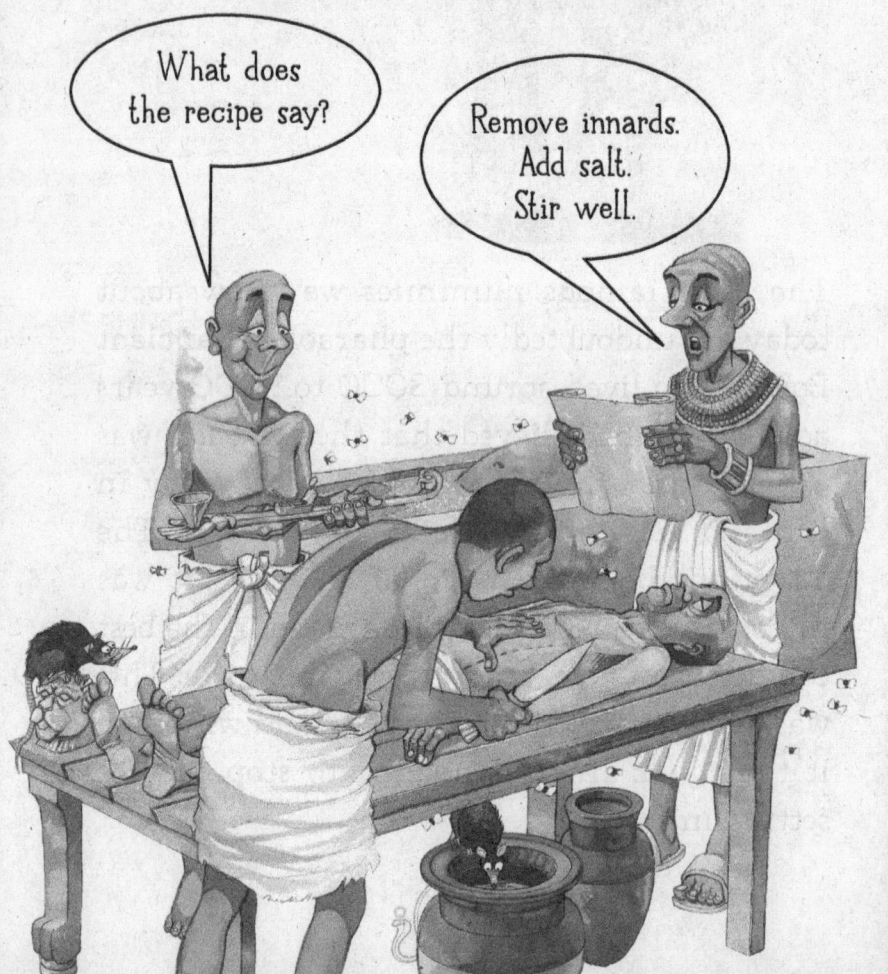

The Egyptians believed dead leaders and their families had to be mummified by an expert team of mummy-makers. Here's their recipe:

1 Take one dead pharaoh and give it a good scrub.

2 Remove all the organs, apart from the heart.

3 Poke a long hook up the nose and mash the brain. Pull out goo through nostrils.

4 After 40 days stuff with cloth and sawdust.

5 Cover body in oils and wrap with long cloth strips.

6 Place in stone coffin called a sarcophagus, seal tightly and leave to stand forever.

7 Lie back and imagine a perfect afterlife... being admired in a cosy museum.

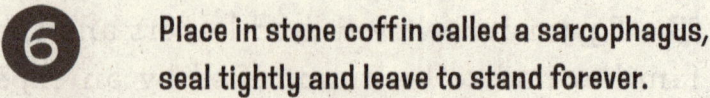

Q: Knock knock.
A: Who's there?
Q: Archie.
A: Archie who?
Q: Archie-ologist looking for a pharaoh's tomb.

Q: What is a Mummy's favourite song?
A: Bohemian Wrapsody

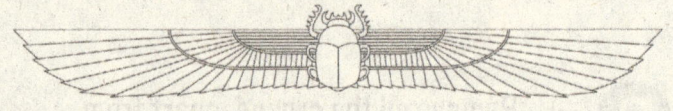

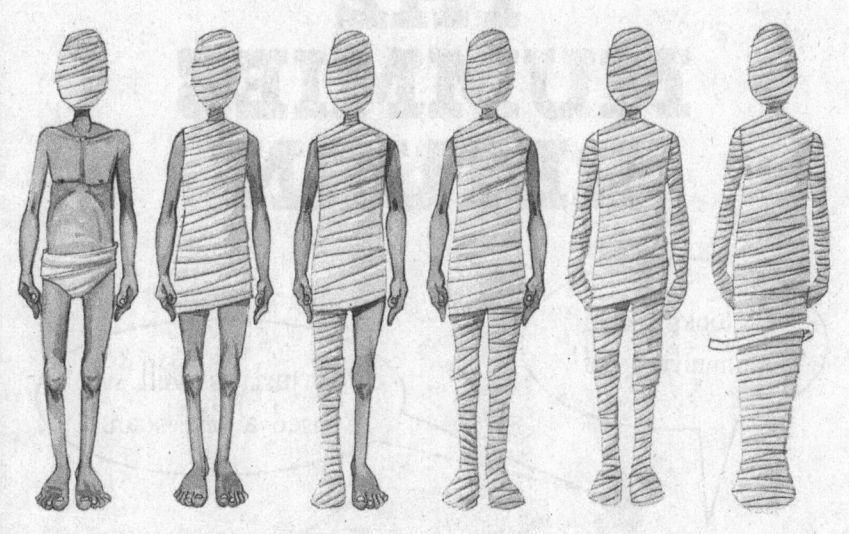

DID YOU KNOW?

Unwrapped, the bandages of an ancient Egyptian mummy could stretch for 1.6 km. That's miles better than just a few strips (actually, that's pretty much one whole mile of bandage).

THE MUMMIES RETURN

THAT'S A WRAP!

As so many artefacts have been stolen from Egypt, the country is keen to get them back. In 2009, 'Operation Mummy's Curse' began to fight the trade in ancient objects, particularly those smuggled into the US.

In fact, a 3,000-year-old stolen mummy hand was found at an American movie studio, where it was used as a prop for actors to wave. You've got to hand it to them though, the studio sent it straight back to Egypt, alongside a mummy's shroud and painted coffins. The Grand Egyptian Museum in Cairo was very pleased to welcome them home.

You may have spotted a mummy on screen if you've watched *Night at the Museum*, which was filmed in the British Museum. Would you dare spend the night alone among the undead?

CAN YOU BELIEVE IT?

When mummy mania spread across Europe, people were desperate to get their hands on them. Fakes flooded the market – the sellers were in de-NILE about the authenticity of their mummies! Even the very first ones to enter the British Museum were found out to be fakes. The first genuine mummies were acquired by the museum in 1756.

I might call in sick today. I'm feeling a bit wrapped up!

CREEPY TALES FROM THE BRITISH MUSEUM...

Most of the mummies in the British Museum still have their wrappings in place, and no mummy has been unwrapped there since the 1790s. One of the British Museum's most famous mummies is nicknamed 'Ginger' because of his unusual hair colour. It actually predates the time Egyptians began mummifying their dead regularly. Ginger was an adult male who died more than 5,000 years ago and was buried in direct contact with the dry desert sand, which is why his body didn't decay. Like many other early Egyptian mummies, he's an example of a natural mummy, created spontaneously through specific environmental conditions. He's also thought to be the oldest.

Like many mummies, Ginger has a creepy tale to tell. The story goes that, when the Museum was looking for a mummy in the 19th century, this specimen was bought from a dodgy dealer. Apparently, the seller had a relative of similar size, stature and appearance to the mummy, who strangely disappeared at the same time Ginger was bought...

However, experts at the British Museum have proven that Ginger is a genuine ancient mummy – and probably a murder victim, too. A scan revealed an injury to Ginger's shoulder blade and a shattered rib underneath, suggesting a stab wound likely killed him.

Thanks to his remarkable preservation, visitors to the museum can now use a touch screen on a virtual operating table to examine Ginger's body and discover clues about his life and death. Why not pop along and meet him?

Unlike fairytales, the lives of ancient Egyptian pharaohs is a tale of riches to rags!

LIVERPOOL MUMMIES

Liverpool's World Museum has over 16,000 objects from ancient Egypt and Nubia, including the mummy of a young boy. It is one of the largest collections in Great Britain. Visitors are invited to explore the special Mummy Room, to read spells from the *Book of the Dead* and even sniff ingredients used in mummification. (No, it's not SPHINX Body Spray).

When the museum's 'Animal Mummies Revealed' exhibition closed in 2017, over 100,000 people had viewed the 60 or so specimens — mummified jackals, crocodiles, birds and, yes, cats. Cat mummies have a particularly grisly history in Liverpool.

It looks like the cat's eaten the budgie.

In 1890, about 180,000 unwrapped feline mummies arrived from Egypt at the city's docks, where they were sold off at auction. At that time, these mummies were not viewed as valuable objects – they had just been used as ballast to balance the ship during the voyage. So who bought them all? Mainly farmers who crushed up the mummies and spread the remains on fields for fertiliser, like manure. If that wasn't bad enough, the auctioneer even used a cat's head as a hammer to strike the sale. But even worse was to come...

NIGHT AT THE MEOWSEUM

A few cat mummies managed to escape such a fate, and were rescued by Liverpool's museum. But they all met a brutal end in World War 2, when the museum was heavily bombed during the blitz. Tragically, the raid destroyed the remaining cat mummies, alongside more than 3,000 Egyptian objects. Maybe it was a mummy's curse at work...

Did you hear about the cat that went into the museum to have her kittens behind a sarcophagus? She was instantly mummified.

When father came to visit, he was instantly daddified. Tee hee.

I hope I don't end up in a purr-amid!

TALKING OF CATS...

Where did all those mummified cats come from?

In 1888, an Egyptian farmer digging in the desert near Istabl Antar fell into a massive grave. But the bodies weren't human. Instead, the tunnel was packed with hundreds of thousands of ancient mummified cats! News soon spread and locals came in search of gold. They found a life-size bronze sarcophagus with a cat inside but apart from that, there were just cats upon cats upon cats. They had been bred in large numbers just to be killed, wrapped in bandages and used as lucky charms to gain favours with the gods.

People descended on the cats mummies, peeling the wrappings off each one then stripping off the brittle fur and piling the bones in black heaps. The rags and other crumbly bits were carted off in donkey loads to be spread on the fields as fertiliser. CATastrophic, or what?

Looks like I've fallen into a CATacomb!

BACK AT THE MUSEUMS...

Just imagine coming face to face with somebody (yes, some body) who is thousands of years old. You can do just that, as well as admire some of their amazing possessions, in lots of British museums, up and down the country.

Archeologists say that mummies are hard to find – they're always kept under wraps!

The National Museum of Scotland in Edinburgh has a very impressive collection, discovered in Egyptian tombs long ago. The museum houses two particularly interesting mummies: a young woman and child, buried with magnificent gold and luxurious finery around 1550 BC. Her stunning gold painted coffin suggests that the woman may have been a queen. Now known as 'The Qurna Queen', she wore a magnificent collar of gold rings, a pair of gold earrings, two pairs of gold bracelets and a girdle of rings (over 90% pure gold). To stop her getting hungry in the afterlife, she was buried with bread, grapes, dates and a pomegranate. Alas, these are now a tad past their sell-by date!

You can even see what this tall, elegant woman would have looked like. Experts have scanned her skull to help create make a realistic model of her face. Why don't you visit, take a peek and say hi!

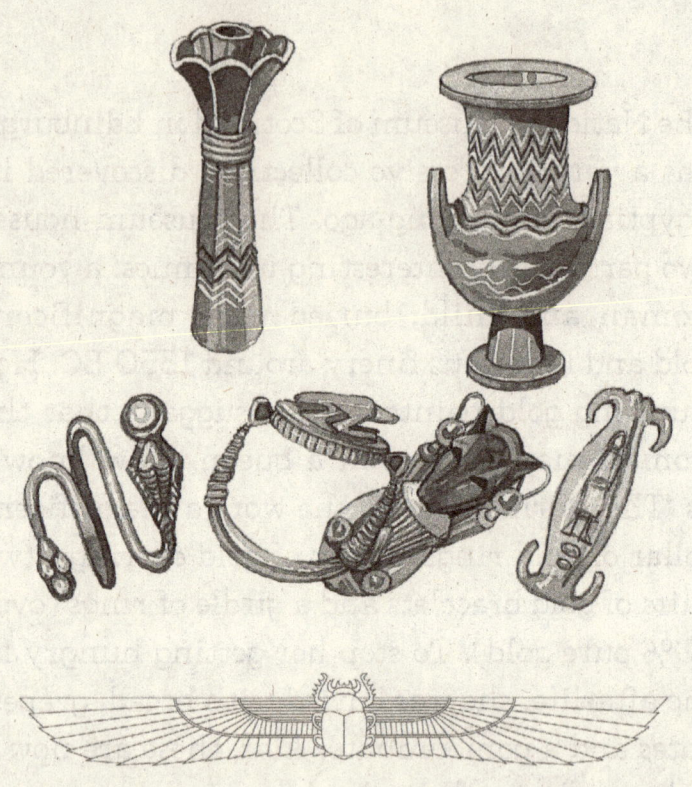

The Egypt Centre in Swansea, South Wales, is home to over 6,000 ancient artefacts, including mummies, weapons, coffins and more. They even possess some ancient earplugs, made from metal discs with grooved edges, which would have been worn on the earlobe as jewellery – rather than as plugs to block out those noisy pyramid builders!

In Northern Ireland, the Ulster Museum has a vast Egyptian collection, including the mummy of an Egyptian aristocrat, Lady Takabuti. Her head is unwrapped, meaning you can actually come face-to-face with someone over 2,700 years old!

It isn't much fun as a mummy,
You could say it's really a bind,
With my bandages yucky and gummy...
How I long to relax and unwind.

IT MUST BE A MUMMY'S CURSE!

Manchester Museum and its amazing Egyptian collection made world news in 2013 when something creepy happened not just in the dead of night... but also in broad daylight! It wasn't anything to do with Asru, the mummy and her coffin nearby, or their collection of mummies from the Roman period. No, this was a little Egyptian statue which began to spin ALL BY ITSELF. It mysteriously started moving very slowly and even scientists were stumped – was it haunted? Yikes!

Q: How do mummies hide?
A: They use masking tape!

A STRANGE TURN OF EVENTS...

Despite being locked up inside its glass case, the statue rotated 180 degrees every three days. The museum's curator kept turning it back, knowing the ancient Egyptians believed that if the mummy was destroyed then the statuette buried alongside it would take on its spirit. A time lapse video showed that the statue was really moving without being touched. Was the mummy's spirit trying to say something?

Scientists suggest the vibrations from footsteps around the room caused the movement, though no other exhibits were affected. The statue also doesn't sit quite flat – it has a little bump on its bottom, which could explain why it took a funny turn!

MUSEUMS OF EGYPT

As you would expect, the most famous (and sometimes scariest) Egyptian mummies can be seen in the city museums of Egypt, such as in Cairo and Luxor.

King Ramses the II (also known as Ramesses the Great) became the ruler of Egypt during his early twenties (around 1279 BC). He ruled for 66 years until his death in 1213 BC – when he was over ninety years old! He was celebrated as one of the greatest, most powerful rulers of the New Kingdom – the golden age of ancient Egyptian rule. In the ancient Greek language, he was called Ozymandias.

Today, the body of the great King Ramses II is one of the best-preserved mummies in the world. He can be found in the Cairo Museum in Egypt. It shows that he stood over six feet tall, with a strong, jutting jaw, thin nose, thick lips and red hair. He suffered from dental problems, severe arthritis and hardening of the arteries, and most probably died from old age or heart failure (not surprising for a man in his mid-nineties with 200 wives!).

The linen over Ramses II's body is covered in hieroglyphics which explain that, after he was first buried in the Valley of the Kings, priests were forced to move the mummy due to avoid rampant looters.

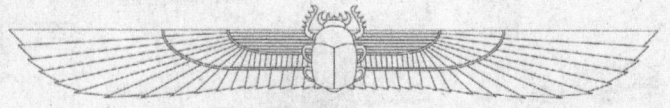

Q: What is it called when a pharaoh is lying in the wrong pyramid?
A: A GRAVE mistake!

MOULDY MUMMIES

About a hundred years after Ramses II's mummy was discovered, archaeologists noticed he was getting a bit mouldy. A gross fungal infection was spreading across his body, so off to the doctors he went! Yes, at the whopping age of around 3,300 years, the mummy was flown over to Paris in 1976. The great pharaoh even had to be given an Egyptian passport, in which his occupation was listed as 'King (deceased)'. You'll be pleased to know the treatment was successful, and he returned to Cairo a lot healthier – and less smelly.

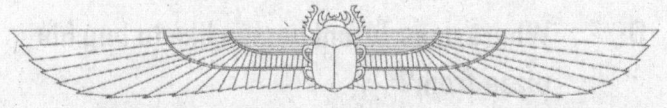

Q: Why did the pharaoh have to go to the dentist?

A: Egypt his tooth! (He chipped his tooth).

TUTANKHAMUN

Probably the most famous pharaoh around was the Egyptian boy king, King Tut, better known as Tutankhamun. He's an ancient icon for a number of reasons: his stunning golden death mask is considered a masterpiece of Egyptian art; his tomb treasures have toured the globe, with millions getting a glimpse of the boy king's vast riches; and his chilling mummy's curse continues to captivate audiences old and new. Tutanmania has swept the world!

Q: Where does Tutankhamun like to buy his pizza from?

A: Pizza Tut!

In 1922 Howard Carter, a British archaeologist, discovered a tomb in The Valley of the Kings. Hidden inside was the mummy of Tutankhamun, surrounded by treasures. Tutankhamun died in about 1324 BC aged around 19, after reigning for nine years. His magnificent solid gold funeral mask is encrusted with lapis lazuli and semi-precious stones. The restored mask is on display at the Egyptian Museum in Cairo.

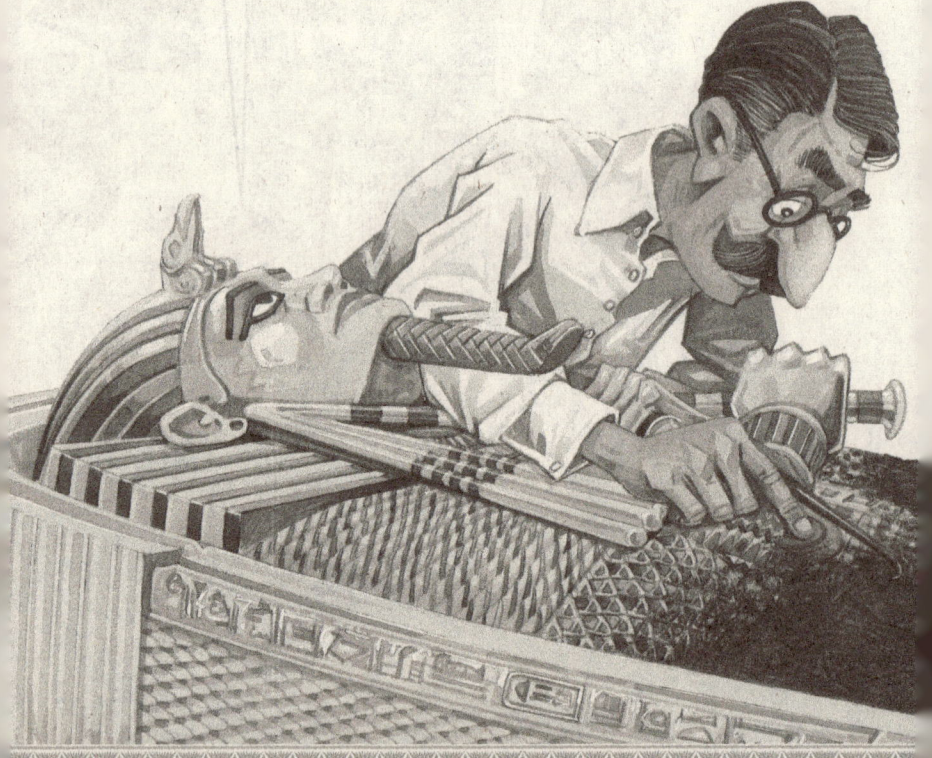

In 2007, 85 years to the day since it was discovered, Tutankhamun's mummy went on display for the first time in his underground tomb at Luxor. Although all the treasures from the tomb have been removed, the mummy itself had been kept in its sarcophagus in the burial chamber. The boy king was finally brought out of hiding and put on public display for all to see. His linen-wrapped mummy is displayed in a special climate-controlled glass box.

WHAT HAPPENED TO KING TUT?

Historians have never been sure how or why Tutankhamun died so young. Some said a hole in the mummy's skull suggested murder. He also had broken bones. Other experts hypothesise that he was killed by a hippopotamus, as Ancient Egyptians hunted hippos for sport. Statues found in the tomb depict King Tut throwing a harpoon, so maybe he was killed in a hunting accident. Then again, he may have been killed by a chariot crashing into him. It's hard to be sure because he wasn't mummified properly; his body cooked and burned due to all the oils used on him. His flesh stuck to the inside of the coffin, so getting him out caused a bit of a mess.

There were many mysteries and myths about Tutankhamun in both life and death. Lord Carnarvon, who funded the excavation in 1922, died suddenly soon afterwards. As he died, the lights in Cairo failed and his dog back home howled. Superstitious people claimed that a curse was at work. Then, in 1944, a tomb robber reached into another coffin to steal some gold. The lid fell and trapped him, before the roof collapsed and killed him. They know the date that he died because that day's newspaper was recovered from his skeleton's tattered coat. Was this the mummy's revenge?

DID YOU KNOW?

Treasures from Tutankhamun's tomb have travelled all across the world. An exhibition in The British Museum in 1972 was attended by 1.6 million visitors, making it the most popular exhibition in the museum's history. The 1977–79 exhibition in the US was attended by over 8 million people. The most popular object from the tomb was the golden death mask topped by a cobra and vulture.

Today you can see (and smell) something of Tutankhamun in Dorchester, England. An exhibition recreated the treasures using mainly the same materials and methods, making them as close as possible to the originals now in Egypt. A reconstruction of the tomb itself has a whiff of history about it, as the creators have recreated the smells that Carter described on finding the tomb. You could say it's more like a 'phew-seum'!

What's King Tut's favourite food?

King Tut-key fried chicken.

Q: How do you open the door at the Cairo Museum?
A: Toot-and-come-in!

MUMMIES AND CURSES

During the 19th century, following the discovery of the first tombs in Egypt, there was huge interest across Europe in Egyptology. Victorian Britain couldn't get enough of mummy-mania. Wealthy people would even hold mummy parties to impress their friends. That's right, they would buy a real mummy, invite their guests over, lower the lights and unwrap it right in front of everyone. No doubt there were squeals of horror or even delight – but sadly, such parties destroyed hundreds of mummies forever. Exposing the ancient remains to the air caused them to fall apart.

Q: What subject did the Pharaoh study in college?

A: Cryptography!

Even more terrible were stage shows held in London theatres, where the tension was built up with gruesome tales of 'the pharaoh's curse' just as a mummy was dramatically unwrapped in front of gasping audiences. The horror of these tasteless public 'undressings', with little respect for the dead, probably inspired scary stories of mummy revenge. Years later, horror movies kept up the idea of mummies striking back, and now mummy costumes at Halloween terrify us along with zombies and ghosts!

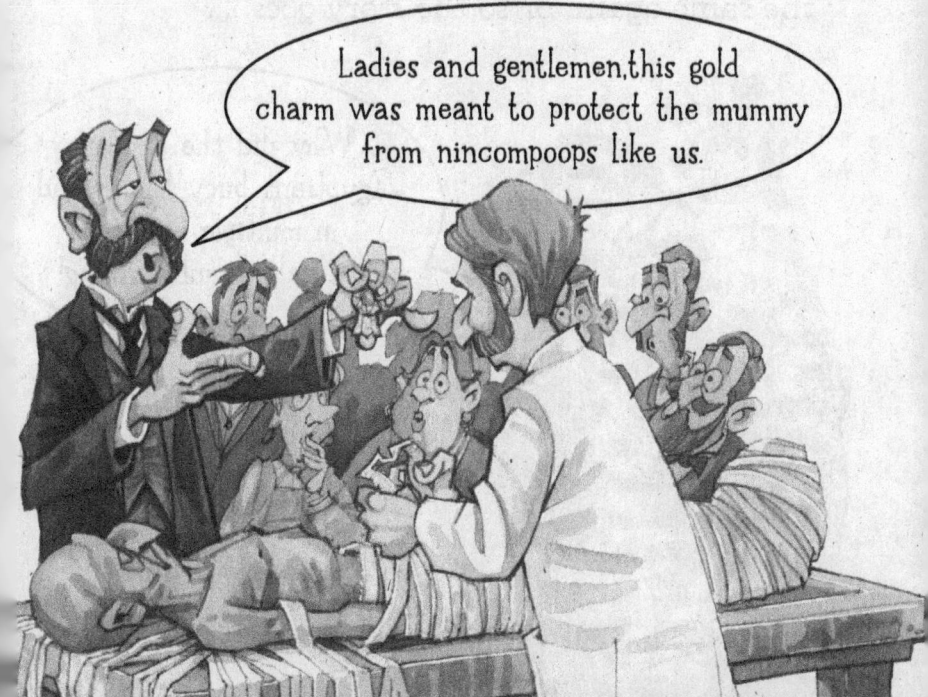

Ladies and gentlemen, this gold charm was meant to protect the mummy from nincompoops like us.

THE BRITISH MUSEUM'S CURSED MUMMY

In one of the British Museum's Egypt Rooms, you can see item 22542 – if you dare. Those who cast their eyes on this object may never be the same again, or so the story goes...

Why did the ancient Egyptians bury their dead in multiple coffins? It's called multicasking!

Among the shadowy sarcophagi, bandaged bodies and statues of antiquated deities, you will find yourself staring into the eyes of an ancient face – not a mummy, but a beautifully painted wooden coffin lid of an unidentified woman, around 3,000 years old. She is both fascinating and foreboding, instilling onlookers with an ominous feeling of discomfort. The mummy herself is missing and no one knows where she is or who she was. Some have theorised that she may have been a high priestess of the Temple of Amen-Ra, or an ancient Egyptian princess. And maybe – just maybe – she placed a curse on what became called 'The Unlucky Mummy', which was acquired by the British Museum in 1889.

According to myth and legend, 'The Unlucky Mummy' has mysteriously found herself at the centre of several tragic events since her initial discovery. Sudden death has haunted those who have handled the relic, trailing her journey to the British Museum.

THE MYTH OF 'THE UNLUCKY MUMMY'

After the luxury liner, the *Titanic,* sank in 1912, an unlucky mummy's curse was whispered to be responsible for the disaster. The myth goes something like this:

Happy Mummy's Day!

The mummy-board was said to have been purchased by a young English traveller who visited the archaeological digs in Egypt. He arranged for the coffin to be shipped back to his home, but was not there to receive it. Instead, he and his friends on the same trip all found unfortunate ends: two died or were seriously injured in shooting accidents, and two died after losing their fortune and descending into poverty.

Upon the coffin's arrival in England, it was passed along to one of the traveller's sisters. As soon as it entered her house however, the occupants reported experiencing a series of unfortunate events. Hiring a clairvoyant, an 'evil influence' was reportedly traced back to the mummy-board, and the sister was urged to dispose of 'The Unlucky Mummy' to prevent anymore misfortune. It was therefore presented to the British Museum.

Where do mummies go swimming? The DEAD sea!

The staff at the museum reported hearing loud banging and crying noises coming from the coffin at night. Things were thrown around the exhibit room without explanation. After a guide in the room died suddenly, a photographer took a photo of the coffin. When he developed it, the image that appeared was so horrifying that the photographer leapt from a window!

Believing it to be cursed, the museum now wanted to get rid of the unlucky mummy – and fast! So, it was swiftly sold off to an American archaeologist, who shipped it to the United States aboard the *Titanic*.

I'm sure you can guess what happened next...

They said women and children leave first ... I guess that includes mummies?!

ANY TRUTH TO THE TALE?

Shipping records prove that there was no mummy onboard the *Titanic*. No survivor has ever mentioned sharing a lifeboat with a mummy or coffin! Aside from that, 'The Unlucky Mummy' has been safely tucked up in the British Museum since 1889. But maybe this myth had a grain of truth...

Long ago, two Englishmen claimed to know someone with an ancient Egyptian mummy in his home. The next morning every breakable item in the room had been smashed to pieces. The next night, the mummy was left in another room and the same happened.

When the men saw the coffin lid in the British Museum, they they linked it to their friend's odd experience. They sold the tale to the newspapers and it grew to include the *Titanic* myth.

Perhaps 'The Unlucky Mummy' myth has been intertwined with aspects of a story connected to pharaoh Menkaure's sarcophagus. In 1838, the coffin was placed on a ship called the *Beatrice* on its way to the British Museum, but the ship sadly sank to the bottom of the ocean, and the treasure has never been recovered...

MUMMIES ON THE MARKET

For wealthy American and European tourists in the 19th century, Egypt was the place to visit. Bringing home a mummy as a souvenir to keep in the living room or even the bedroom was seen as very stylish. Mummy hands, feet and heads were frequently displayed around the house, often on the mantelpiece. One Chicago store apparently displayed a mummy said to be a 'Pharaoh's daughter who discovered Moses in the bulrushes'.

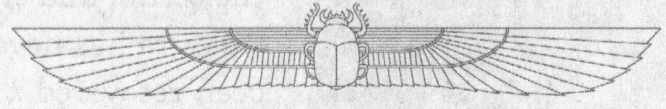

Q: Why couldn't the mummy finish his meal?
A: Because he was stuffed!

MASHED-UP MUMMIES

Can you believe that people used to sprinkle powdered mummy into hot water and drink it? Some people were convinced this medicine would cure all kinds of ailments. A quick swig of mummy broth was thought to do you the world of good (please don't try this next time you have a cold – it could give you a sore-cough-or-gas!)

Can someone give me a hand?

MUMMIES IN CHINA

Ancient mummies have also been found in tombs in China, where they have revealed all kinds of secrets. One 3,600-year-old mummy of a woman shows that she'd received brain surgery — or at least a hole drilled into her skull, which had begun to heal.

Another mummy was the wife of a Chinese ruler. She is known as Lady Dai and she died about 2,200 years ago. Scans showed that she died from a heart attack at 50 years of age due to obesity. When her mummy was examined, she still had moist skin, her joints were still flexible and even her eyelashes and the hair in her nostrils remained. Lady Dai was found in an airtight tomb 12 metres (40 feet) underground, locked inside four layers of coffins. Her body had been buried in 20 layers of silk.

MUMMIES IN SOUTH AMERICA

2,000 years before the Egyptians started mummification, the Chinchorro people, who lived on the coast of the Atacama Desert in South America (Peru and Chile today) were already mummifying their dead people. The oldest Chinchorro mummies date back about 7,000 years. The dead bodies had their organs removed, their skin was sewed back and their bodies were painted black from head to toe. Then the Chinchorro people would place wigs on the heads, and they left the eyes and mouths open. Some even had tattoos. Unfortunately, some on display in Arica Museum in Chile are going black, slimy, oozy and squidgy. After all, you can't expect anyone to be at their best at 7,000 years old!

BOG MUMMIES

If you happen to visit the National Museum of Ireland in Dublin, you could come face-to-face with some 'natural' mummies, known as the 'bog people'. One of the most famous bog bodies on show in Dublin is the Cashel Man, who was discovered in Cashel bog, County Laois in 2011. Incredibly, he had been there for 4,000 years and was preserved in the peat! The bog's unique conditions, such as highly acidic water, limited oxygen and low temperatures, created an effective enviornment for preservation.

Archaeologists have been able to study the mummy to discover more about life in the Bronze Age. He may have ruled as king of his region once, and met his violent, bloody end at the hands of his subjects – historians believe he was likely murdered or sacrificed after a series of poor harvests.

ICE MUMMIES

High in the Alps of Austria, hikers discovered a frozen body in 1991. This 'ice mummy' was 5,300 years old and he's now known as Otzi. You can see him and his belongings at the South Tyrol Museum of Archaeology in Bolzano, Italy. But now there are more of him! His mummy has been scanned and 3D printed, to create three life-size Ötzi clones. The Iceman's first two 3D prints are on display at the DNA Learning Center in New York. The third life-size print is in a travelling exhibit, making Otzi quite a celebrity.

Another famous frozen mummy is the Siberian Ice Maiden, better known as the Ukok Princess. This 2,500-year-old lady who died in her twenties is well-known for her stunning tattoos, which are said to be the most elaborate of their kind anywhere on Earth.

But not everyone was happy about removing her from her icy tomb. Local people believe a curse was unleashed when her body was disturbed. Forest fires, earthquakes and illnesses have been blamed on her mummy. Yet scientists believe that they have gained amazing historical knowledge from her remains. Even so, the fear of an icy curse still looms for some of those who discovered the mummy...

Don't you think my tattoos are INK-credible?

In 1995, high in the Andes Mountains of Peru, a volcano melted the ice that had preserved 'the ice maiden', now called Juanita. She was about 12-14 years old when she died 500 years ago – probably killed as a sacrifice to please the Inca gods.

If you'd like to say hello to Juanita, she and 13 similar mummies are rotated and displayed in a glass container at -20°C in the Arequipa Museum in Peru. You'd better wear a thick vest though –
it's chilly!

'PLASTER MUMMIES' OF VESUVIUS

When the Italian volcano Vesuvius erupted in AD 79, the gas and ash that poured from the crater killed thousands of people in nearby Pompeii and Herculaneum.

People were going about their daily lives, then suddenly they were preserved in an instant. Their bodies were buried in ash. When archaeologists began digging into the ash, they discovered people-shaped holes that were once the victim's bodies. By pouring liquid plaster into these holes, scientists have been able to make detailed casts of the citizens of ancient Pompeii. Many visitors go to see these 'plaster mummies' at the Antiquarium Museum, which is just up the street from the Porta Marina entrance to Pompeii. You can see mummy-like statues of men, women, children and animals that lived nearly 2,000 years ago.

MUSEUMS WITH A HEAD START

Some mummies aren't really mummies. They're just preserved heads that have been shrunk. You can sometimes see these gruesome objects in museums which display how other cultures once lived.

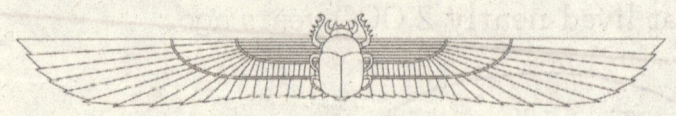

The Pitt Rivers Museum in Oxford, UK is like a packed warehouse of all kinds of treasures — but be warned of what you might meet down one of the shadowy aisles. Yes, you could come head to head with a shrunken head.

The many shrunken heads that are on display in the Pitt Rivers Museum are originally from the Upper Amazon region of South America. They were created by the Shuar and Achuar peoples, who still live in the dense Amazonian jungle. Men from these tribes kept enemy heads to capture souls and keep their power for their own people. You'll be relieved to know these people no longer kill enemies, cut off their heads and shrink them, and haven't done so since the 1960s!

SHRUNKEN HEADS

This was how it was done (look away now!):

1 Skin the head, throwing away the skull and brain.

2 Soak the skin in hot water, then pour in hot sand.

3 Repeat the hot sand treatment several times over a period of months.

4 Mould the nose and cheeks after each treatment.

5 Sew the eyes and mouth closed with cotton string.

6 Blacken the face with vegetable dye to prevent the soul from escaping and seeking revenge on the killer.

7 String the heads on a cord and wear at ritual feasts!

GRUESOME GIFTS

European explorers collected shrunken heads as souvenirs. Those at the Pitt Rivers Museum were collected between 1871 and 1936. At that time, many fake heads were made from monkey or goat heads. Some were even made from unclaimed human bodies in morgues and hospitals. Fortunately, times have changed for the better!

Q: What is the best job for a mummy during the holidays?

A: A gift wrapper!

Today, lots of thought goes into museum exhibitions, especially when displaying human remains. The Pitt Rivers Museum often considers whether the way such objects are displayed is respectful, and tries to make the information 'appropriate and clearly communicated'.

Even so, whoever would want to spend a night alone in the room with the shrunken heads?

It would do your head in.

To do well at school, just visit the museum to get a head...

MUMMIFIED AND RATIFIED

Rat 1: The Egyptians mummified a lot of rats, you know.

Rat 2: Are you sure?

Rat 1: Yes – many rat mummies had little coffins, too.

Rat 2: Whatever for?

These fleas are getting me ratty!

Rat I: To keep them safe for the afterlife.
It was believed that rats ate the hearts of
sinners on judgment day.

Rat 2: Yuk!

Rat I: And did you know that the pharaohs were
mummified with their hands crossed over
their chests?

Rat 2: I wonder why?

Rat I: Maybe they thought there would be lots
of water slides in the afterlife. Tee hee!

I'm just worn out,
that's all. Life's a rat
race right now.

AN ANCIENT EGYPTIAN VERSION OF TV'S MASTERCHEF

Featuring presenters Gregg & John, and contestants Nef & Seti

Gregg: Welcome to Master Mummy, where our contestants this week have the mother of all challenges...

John: Or rather the mummy of all challenges. They've got to prepare a real mummy. It could get messy – but it's no good going crying to mummy!

Gregg: Yes, they both have to make a mummy using similar ingredients. So who will we be sending home today?

John: It's a competition to prepare the best mummy in ancient Egypt. So welcome to the wabet. It's where Egyptian bodies get prepared to become mummies. Let's meet the contestants...

Nef: Hello, I'm Nef. I'm very nervous but I think I can do this even though I'm squeamish.

Gregg:	Well good luck, Nef. I hope you can rise to today's challenge. Who will you be mummifying for us today?
Nef:	My mother-in-law – or as I now call her: Mummy-in-law.
John:	Great! Let's meet contestant number two.
Seti:	Hello, I'm Seti. I've never made a mummy before but I've bandaged up my granny a few times so it should be breeze. I've just got a dead pharaoh delivered. He's still quite fresh and I'm raring to go.
John:	Don't forget to use a wooden tag to label your mummies. We don't want any mummy mix-ups when we pop them in the pyramid tomb in a sarcophagus.
Gregg:	So it just remains for us to start the clock. Both contestants are now at their

slabs, each with a body stretched in front of them, with a range of the best ingredients and natron salt for making a master mummy. The bodies have already had a good soak in natron solution for just over a month, so they're nice and dried out – like a piece of papyrus!

John: You have just thirty minutes to mummify. May the best mummy win. GO!

Narrator: Nef is making a cheap 'basic range' mummy, using a cedar oil infusion, alongside a natron dressing and a light drizzle of perfume.

Nef: (Dabbing perfume on herself) Silly to waste this on mother-in-law now.

Narrator: Seti is preparing a mid-range mummy for only a mid-range pharaoh. The body has just been delivered from the 'ibu' tent of purification and the organs are about to be removed for pickling. Seti will be serving the mummy in a linen wrap and a spicy frankincense syrup on a bed of papyrus leaves.

Seti: (Squeezing out a wet rag) Firstly a quick wash with a solution of natron dissolved in water. (Washes own arms while consulting a recipe book covered in hieroglyphics) Oops, wrong body!

Gregg: Tell me what you're doing, Nef.

Nef: I'm using a slicer to cut open the body so that the organs can be removed for drying out. I'll need to use this clothes peg, too.

Gregg: For hanging up the organs to dry?

Nef: No, to put on my nose. It's a smelly
           job. I'm just taking out the liver, lungs,
           stomach and intestines. Phew!

Gregg: That's very brave of you.

Nef: Yes, I've got a lot of guts. With this gross
           recipe, you can easily get upset.

Gregg: So you've got to be heartless?

Nef: Certainly not – I've kept the heart inside.
           It will be needed in the afterlife.

John: Tell us what you're doing with all the other organs, Nef.

Nef: I've popped them in canopic jars with images of the gods.

Narrator: Nef is washing out the body's inside with palm wine, then soaking it in more natron to dry out.

Gregg:	Tell us what you're doing, Seti.
Seti:	I'm making a very fine brain mash with this special tool I call a nose-pick. I just pop it up the pharaoh's nose like this... And when it reaches the brain, I just give it a little P.S.M.S.
John:	Professional Skill and Medical Science?
Seti:	No – Push, Squeeze, Mince and Squelch. The brain shoots out down the nose in one gooey mess. Are you all right?
John:	I think I'm going to be sick... (runs off)
Gregg:	Hurry, you need to be wrapping your bodies in bandages by now. Normally this should need twenty layers of linen over fifteen days.

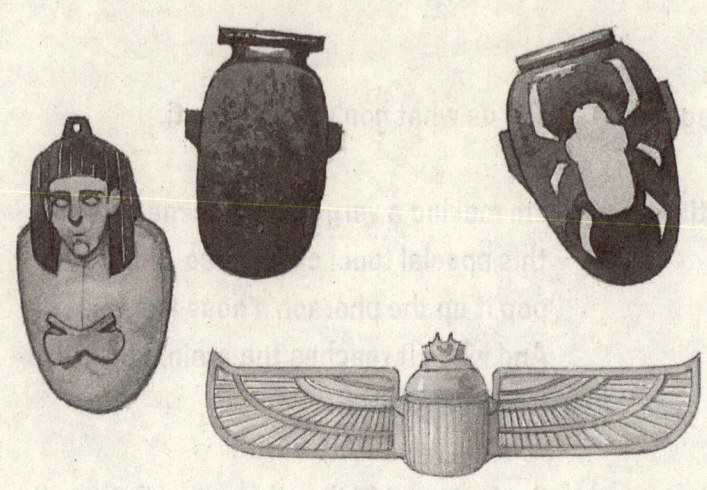

Narrator:	Nef is tucking little amulets into the bandages.
Nef:	This is a scarab amulet, which is a lucky charm. It's for stopping my mummy's secrets getting found out.
John:	You both have ten seconds left to complete your mummy...
Narrator:	Nef is still tangled up in bandages.

Nef: I think I've finished. It's a wrap!

Gregg: Five seconds left.

Narrator: Seti has forgotten to put the heart back in, which is very important for the pharaoh in the afterlife.

Gregg: Stop! Stand back from your mummies.

John: Nef, I like your style. Neat bandaging here, just a few frayed edges but most parts sealed and wrapped.

Gregg: Seti, a mad panic to get the heart back in there but you just about did it.

John: To me, you've overdone the resin. The oils are coming over too strong. You don't want a Tutankhamun to happen, do you?

Nef: What's that?

John: He got mummy-fried. The embalming oils in Tutankhamun's mummy caught fire inside the sarcophagus and he cooked. Barbecued mummy isn't nice.

It's best to take all this nonsense with a pinch of salt.

Narrator: So, who goes on to the next round?
              Which mummy will be going home on the
              bus? The judges are about to make their
              decision.

Gregg: One of you will be going through to the
              next round. One of you is about to be sent
              home. (Scary music)

John: The one of you going home is...
              (VERY long pause)

Gregg: Did I just hear you swear, Nef?

Nef: It wasn't me, honest.

Gregg: Yikes – in that case... It's 'The Mummy's
              Curse'!

(Sudden scary laugh. Both mummies sit up and do
triumphant high-fives as sinister music plays and
everyone runs off, screaming!)

Egyptian Mummy (on phone):
Hello, I'd like to reserve a table for the pharaoh Sakhrakhotep.

Restaurant:
Could you spell that, please?

Egyptian Mummy:
Of course. Bird, two triangles, wavy line, the sun, bird again, jackal's head and a scarab.

Q: What did the Pharaoh say when he woke up and realised he had been mummified?

A: Nothing, his tongue was in a separate jar!

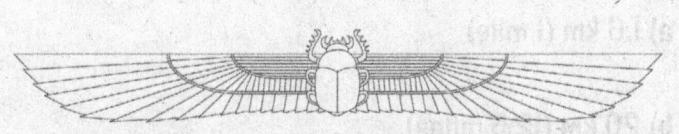

THE MUMMY MANIA QUIZ

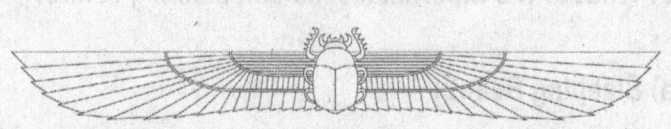

1. How far could the unwrapped bandages of an Egyptian mummy stretch?

a) 1.6 km (1 mile)

b) 20 km (12.5 miles)

c) 2.5 km (1.5 miles)

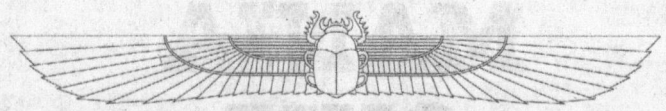

2. What is the Siberian ice maiden mummy called?

a) Sleeping Beauty

b) Ukok Princess

c) Frostina

3. What was the name of the operation to prevent the trade in smuggled Egyptian artefacts?

a) Operation Mummy's Curse

b) Operation Ramesses' Revenge

c) Operation Sarcophagus Stakeout

4. Which museum in Oxford, UK has shrunken heads in its collection?

a) Ashmolean Museum

b) Pitt Rivers Museum

c) Oxford Museum of Natural History

5. What is the name of the scary-looking mummy of a young man in Cairo Museum?

a) The Moaning Mummy

b) The Screaming Mummy

c) The Wailing Mummy

6. What did Howard Carter discover in 1922?

a) A new element in the periodic table

b) Cleopatra's wig

c) The tomb of Tutankhamun

7. What was Cashel Man's body naturally preserved in?

a) A bog

b) Quicksand

c) Vinegar

8. What colour hair did Ramses the Second have?

a) Red

b) Blue

c) Brown

9. Which Chinese mummy was found in an airtight tomb, 12 metres (40 feet) underground?

a) Lady Lin

b) Lady Lulu

c) Lady Dai

10. What is the name of the people who lived in the Atacama desert and painted their mummies' bodies black?

a) Chinchorro

b) Chinchin

c) Cheesy

Answers:

GLOSSARY

Archaeologist: a person who studies excavated sites and artefacts to find out about past civilisations.

Bacteria: microscopic lifeforms, which are usually single-celled and often cause disease.

The Blitz: the nighttime bombing raids carried out by Germany against London and other cities in Britain during the Second World War.

Book of the Dead: an ancient Eyptian text containing spells that were supposed to help a person get into the afterlife.

Cairo: a 1000-year-old Egyptian city, and the capital of modern-day Egypt.

Canopic jars: special containers that held the organs of a mummy, including the lungs, liver, intestines and stomach.

Egyptologist: an archaeologist who specialises in studying the artefacts and ruins of Ancient Egypt.

Fertiliser: a substance, rich in nutrients, added to soil to make it more fertile and capable of growing crops.

GIGGLE GURU

Hieroglyphics: the Egyptian writing system, with an alphabet of stylised pictures or symbols.

Mummy: A dead body that has been preserved through either intentional methods of embalming or environmental factors.

Pharaoh: The divine, supreme ruler of Ancient Egypt.

Pyramids: Giant four-sided monuments built as burial vaults for the pharaohs of Anicent Egypt. They were made from stone and sloped to a point at the top.

Rosetta stone: A special stone slab discovered in 1799. It is inscribed with hieroglyphics, demotic characters and Ancient Greek. The stone is part of a larger slab, and became a very valuable key in deciphering hieroglyphics.

Sphinx: A mythological animal with the body of a lion and the head of a human. Stone sphinxes were built to guard tombs.

Sarcophagus: A stone coffin, often decoratively adorned.

Valley of the Kings: the burial site of many pharaohs of Ancient Egypt, located to the west of the River Nile in Upper Egypt.

GIGGLE GURU

I tickled my brain with Egyptian excitement, hilarious history, and pharaoh funnies. Having conquered the quiz, I'm now a proven pro on all things Ancient Egypt!

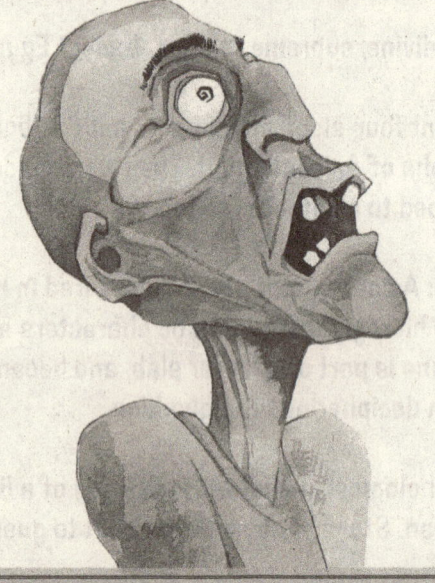

Name:

....

Date:

.........../.........../..........